11/30/06

Happy Birthday, Robbie, and thank you for helping to bring these poems to life.

John

The Musician, Approaching Sleep

Poems by
J. Morris

Dos Madres Press
P.O. Box 294, Loveland, Ohio 45140
http://www.dosmadres.com
editor@dosmadres.com

Dos Madres is dedicated to the belief that the small press is essential to the vitality of contemporary literature as a carrier of the new voice, as well as the older, sometimes forgotten voices of the past. And in an ever more virtual world, to the creation of fine books pleasing to the eye and hand.

Dos Madres is named in honor of Vera Murphy and Libbie Hughes, the "Dos Madres" whose contributions have made this press possible.

Executive Editor: Robert J. Murphy

Book Design & Illustration by Elizabeth Murphy
(IllusionStudios.net)

Typeset in Adobe Garamond Pro
& Aquiline

ACKNOWLEDGMENTS

Grateful acknowledgment is made to the following publications, in which some of these poems first appeared: *Acumen, The Christian Science Monitor, Cumberland Poetry Review, Evansville Review, Möbius, Number One, Other Poetry, Slant, Southwestern American Literature, The Sow's Ear Poetry Review, Willow Review,* and *Yankee.*

Copyright 2006 Dos Madres Press
ISBN 1-933675-15-2

Table of Contents

The Page-Turner 1

The Lodger 3

Power Outage 6

The Musician, Approaching Sleep 8

On Meaning 9

Doctoring the House 10

Divorce 11

Born in 1984 12

Letter to a Friend 13

Civilization and Its Discontents 15

Field 16

Answer to Simmias 17

The Page-Turner

is understood to be invisible,

perched beyond the lowest octave,
poised, a tense handmaiden, eyes
faithful to the score, ready to release
the hands clenched

prayerfully in her lap. Pizzicato
cello-strings quiver. Violin-
and viola-bows leap up, a trio of shuttles
warp-weaving,

the pianist's fingers threading the weft.
Now the notes are running out of room,
she leans, then she thrusts
a bare arm out

into the loom's fabric, her fingers
seize the recto corner and freeze.
Perilous moment! We are not meant to notice
her, the rapt gaze

fastened on her maestro's face,
waiting for that cue, impersonal --
curt nod, lofted eyebrow, even a deeper
breath -- that gives

permission to the page-turner, that says
Now I need you!, and she performs
so swiftly, all elegance and clarity
in the turning,

accomplished. Then tacet once more,
waiting, returned beyond the lowest
possibility of sound, to listen,
to watch. As we watch

what is woven yet can't be seen,
the beauty calling the quintet
and us to gather -- all unseen.
We go home,

make our customary mistakes, confuse
visible signs with invisible grace.
But as sleep deranges us, perhaps
we hear the tapestry

and glimpse a silent turning of the page.

The Lodger

She sensed a figure in the room.
Before the lamp went out, a poem

had inched across her memory,
from early in the century,

when she was young. *I am dreaming.*
The light was gathered in the room

unevenly, a little here,
and there thicker. The comforter

fell from her fingertips, speech
impossible.   She saw a thatch

of grizzled hair above his parts,
as the light moved with him in the dark,

she saw his chin, bare knobby chest,
belly. *My lodger's mad.* Her sense

of what was light and what was dark
abandoned her. Now she could talk.

She said his name.
   They were both eighty.
Daily greetings, rent paid

the month's first morning, in cash.
A that's-done nod from his neat mustache,

and he took himself back down the hall
and shut his door. Their mutual

respect for privacy was not petty
or rigid. She didn't mind the Verdi

operas he liked to play,
always the same ones, identically

scratched and pocked, and his lips pressed
tight -- *I could say much!* -- as he kibitzed

from East to North to West to Dummy,
circling her weekly foursome.

    She said his name, but he only took
a small step closer -- the floor spoke --

changing what was light and what
was not. *Was not. My lodger's mad,*

his lips pale, yet so imploring,
as if, by taking off his clothing

and crossing the hall and letting the light
touch him in wrinkled, pale, private

places, he meant to ask a question.
She felt no fear at all.
                      At breakfast

she served his coffee, offered cream
and asked him how he'd slept. "I dreamed,"

he said, and sipped. Frowning, he stopped.
She watched him place the sloshing cup

back in its saucer, touch the knot of
his dark green tie.
                      She called his daughter

and on the first of the following month
she had no lodger. Surely death

would take him soon, out of the Home.
Vivid at night, poem after poem

returned to her. She felt her youth
retrieve itself. Surely death

would send him naked through the air
to haunt her. She started to prepare.

Power Outage

What I tell you in darkness, that speak ye in light.

God's personal supply -- lightning
thrown down with the twilight rain --
cancels mine. But nothing personal:
He's playing indiscriminate Zeus,
the whole block's gone dark. Mister Coffee
is brain-dead, so Robbie's made

a caffeine run to Starbucks while I wait,
broody on our screened porch, denied
the electric pleasures of books,
music, writing. Wisps of silvery cat-hair
drift against the screen, wanting out:
a fair synecdoche of *cat*. Beyond the hedge,

children laugh in the wet street,
cheering the slickered Virginia Power men.
Trills and hoots spit like sparks from the trees,
a current of cadential urgency: bird-calls:
still I can't make out a single response
amid the stretto of avian babble.

My cat's grave is half-dug: pick clotted with clay,
shovel pebble-nicked, the tools downed until
the storm abates. I held his head, rubbed his yellowed ears and
murmured at his spirit while the vet disorganized the flesh
with one finger firm on the syringe's plunger.
A rheostat steadily turning counterclockwise:
nictitation and breath and pulse dim, diminish, finish.
I stroked the fur of a dead thing,
kept stroking because I had always stroked the fur.

I need coffee and light, immediately.

What I have: absolute certainty
that Virginia Power will fix
the break. Confidence that Robbie
will (barring the unspeakable) splash up
to our curb with the 12 oz cups
in their plastic mobcaps. Beyond these

particular, easy instances of faith,
only a helplessly general mumble --
numbered hairs, the sparrow's fall, Talitha cumi! --
I fear even the birds and children
laugh at, twittering in the approach of dark,
contemptuous of my earth-encrusted tools.

The Musician, Approaching Sleep

After the *lento* loading-out
(which I performed with a firmer touch
at nineteen than I can muster at thirty-nine)
I hunch on the wheel and hug the line.
Good morning; it's three AM from the jock
at the FM mike, ten thousand watts to the west.
I tally a single night's score
of the thousand natural shocks:
my lower back an amplified nest
of bad-tempered wasps, my tympanums deadened
and no doubt damaged, the road unraveling,
full of mist and oncoming drunks. The tide-pull
of sleep. The coffee pissed away.
I struggle to keep myself in sight of the shore.
This is the part they pay me for:
the danger of drowsing out too soon
and never getting back. This is the part
I pay for with a *staccato* heart,

not the moments, earlier,
when the bones in my hands became the sticks
the drummer clutched, and my nerves and fingers got
to know a solo I did not. Music plays
far, far beneath self, like sleep,
like the old joke: where does the light
go when it goes out? Music stops
my self and Maestro Death will do the same.
One aberrant twitch, doing seventy,
one careless lane-switch,
will send me out, *sforzando*. But
all musicians know a safer way
to go out, to go down, to be and not to be,
and play, man, play, play, play.

On Meaning

That name, *Raoul Cedras*.
A beautiful, deceptive combination
of syllables: Ra*oul* dawdles to a close,
dwindles through the narrowing circle, and then
my lips pull back and my tongue attacks
with a sharp, emphatic C*edras*.
I savor the name. The thing named lurks
there, between the rolled *r*'s,
a torturer, machete-proud, a cheater --
but soon to be eliminated from play,
and in ten years' time (I almost wrote *tears*)
his beautiful name will have dwindled away.
Raoul Cedras, Raoul Cedras, I croon and hiss,
cheating the man of meaning. Reducing him to this.

*Raoul Cedras briefly ruled Haiti in the 1990s
before being forced to flee the country.*

Doctoring the House

Chattering, they come for you in the gloom
of dawn. Tarps, chisels, coffee breath.
Hello. Hola. You hide in your highest room,
turn up the Franklin stove, turn up Aretha --
warmth and soul. Drums and horns to drown
the clatter of violent expertise downstairs,
soon. They drape the couch and chairs. They don
their masks. Diligent workers. Urgent repairs.

Someday a specialist will examine *you*,
scare you, then submit his estimate.
You'll give permission, flee upstairs and cower.
Below, respectful masked men will do
damage for good. You may remember it --
the morning all went well? -- at this late hour.

IVORCE

They made the vow at City Hall, Manhattan,
June, forty-six. Ring, license. The JP
invokèd obedience, honor, fidelity
"till death do you part." *I do.* And that was that,
and no one there to cry. The bridegroom lied;
he never meant to honor her. She never
did obey him. They staggered on, tethered
for fifty-four sad, ragged years, and died

eight weeks apart. *They're with each other now
forever,* says the priest. The JP spoke
a kinder truth, I think. The earthly blunder
stopped with Heaven. Death revoked the vow
my parents never kept and never broke.
Let none re-yoke what God has pulled asunder.

 Born in 1984

The girl is seventeen and can't spell
or punctuate or tell the difference
between a complete sentence
and a kind of stutter on the page.

Her take on Winston Smith
is reasonable, she gets him right
because she's obviously bright
and cares and is sensitive about people

and because she has a good teacher
(who has been instructed to ignore
the shambles of language). Her score
on the test will do her, and her parents, proud.

So on to the real world, where it may not matter
much -- or it may, if her job application
gets in the hands of some impatient
old-school pedant, or if her century

turns out to be the one that kills literacy.
No one left to write the books, or read them.
Essential words forgotten; freedoms
too. That will matter, though she can't spell them

and doesn't yet need them.

LETTER TO A FRIEND

Dear J.T.:

In Oxford's cathedral, vaulted and spare,
I lit a candle and muttered a prayer,
gestures that would have meant little to you
in this life. Your gods, if any, were captured in nooks
at the Bodleian Library, chained to the blue-
surrounded spires, spooks
inhabiting history, prompting poetry, haunting books.

Indelible shadow, brutal truncation,
ache in the memory, constant sensation
of sorrow backed up in the throat -- death
is the birth of an absence that wails and feeds and grows stronger
and still is an infant. Imagine the teeth
it will cut, imagine the hunger,
the raging, the years before it grows up and is with me no longer.

In motion, my shiny new ring became part
of the flickering chapel. You died at the start,
last year, of your forty-third year -- my age
to the day, candle in hand. You wandered here
on your honeymoon too, and returned engaged
to Magdalen Bridge, to the queer
wandering arches. You loved the gargoyles, hated the beer.

The infant howled. After I crossed
myself and departed, pound-coin tossed
in the jar for donations, the wax, the wick,
the smoke and the gimcrack flame were hideously small
in the vault of grief. And prayer? -- a trick
or a true chink in the wall.
Surely you know the answer by now. Or know nothing at all.

Gestures that would have meant little to you.
But the effort of crafting the lines, each blue
morning back home, palpating the nooks

of structure to feel for a fitting rhyme: no prayer
could have pleased you like this. Bodley's books
make up a heaven, despair
a gowned scholar praising the quads and towers. Take care.

J.

Civilization and its Discontents

The infant's desires are, in compass, small
(milk, a soothing hand, clean diapers) and carry
no threat to comity. Older children also
are limited in what they might demand --
undeveloped imaginations, too shallow
dredgings of *want* and *need*. No reason not to
free them, more or less, let them enjoy
their tantrums, give them toys, weave stories at bedtime.
(We do well, though, to keep the kittens
safe from their experimental sticks and thumbs.)
But soon, far too soon, a terrible grief:
the capacity for desiring bloats and explodes,
its possible satisfactions multiply,
touch the unknowable, and know neither order
nor decency. Can we picture the full indulgence
of any man's wants, any woman's? All moral fetters
removed, the world lined up and organized
to truly please? Shades of de Sade, of Dachau.
It is so sad, that we are so wrong in ourselves
that stern renunciation becomes both right and
the only practical way to get along.
Shouldn't we, then, pamper the babes, serve them,
rush to respond to each whimpered velleity?
They'll have to stop that nonsense soon enough --
at least allow them the memory of perfect pleasure.
Or would that only make their lives sadder?

Field

A field of black-eyed susans that you ran
through, your shirt off, brassy petals
shining, sun and a sneezy scent, your face
so close to the thousand dark eyes that swayed
unblinking in your wake. Only three years old,
you gave no thought to running through, didn't wonder
what might remain. Yet it does,
the memory glows. Skin, sun, blossoms -- larger,
somehow, than the tall man waiting
at the edge of the field to take you home.

ANSWER TO SIMMIAS

> Simmias, if I remember rightly, has fears and misgivings
> whether the soul, being in the form of harmony,
> although a fairer and diviner thing than the body,
> may not perish first.
>
> Plato, *Phaedo*

This happened to me once: I wrote a chaconne
for orchestra (these were my student days),
I scored the thing, took pains, and heard my phrases
begin to soar above their grounded bass.
And then I lost the pages, God knows how.
Those precious, scribbled staves just disappeared
beneath the waves of senior-year disorder.
I wasn't daunted, though. I could still hear it,
the music in my "head," my "thoughts," my "mind":
unscientific terms: had I dropped dead
that day, the probing scalpels would have failed
to find a single quaver in my brain.
Yet they were there, I heard it, wrote it down
again -- improved it, even, took it closer
to what I had in mind.
                          Now please imagine
your soul as music. You live out your years
becoming rhythm, harmony, the structure
of what you are. Then comes the final measure,
the whole-note rest of death. The printed score --
your blood and bones and breath and DNA --
will decompose, will disappear as quickly
as my first-draft chaconne. What of the music?
How can you live again? A greater mind
must needs remember you and let you play
forever, each thematic line perfected
and finally sounding true. Heaven is sounding
impossible these days, with every quantum
of matter mathematically weighed and accounted for.
But it's no more, or less, miraculous
than what I have in mind.

                              And so, *da capo:*
the choirmaster smiles and gives the downbeat,
the angels pluck you out upon their lyres
while voices far more absolute, more lovely
than any you imagined sing the burden,
as light as life. Simmias, let us pray:
Remember us, O Lord. Keep us in mind.